This book belongs to

....

A gift from

....

Date

....

Visit Tyndale's exciting Web site for kids at www.tyndale.com/kids

TYNDALE is a registered trademark of Tyndale House Publishers, Inc.

Tyndale Kids logo is a trademark of Tyndale House Publishers, Inc.

My Story Bible: 66 Favorite Stories

Copyright © 2008 Anno Domini Publishing

1 Churchgates, The Wilderness, Berkhamsted, Herts HP4 2UB England

Text copyright © 2008 Jan Godfrey

Illustrations copyright © 2008 Paola Bertolini Grudina

Editorial director: Annette Reynolds

Editor: Nicola Bull

Art director: Gerald Rogers

Cover design: Jacqueline L. Nuñez

Pre-production: Krystyna Kowalska Hewitt

Production: John Laister

Library of Congress Cataloging-in-Publication Data

Godfrey, Jan.
  My story Bible : 66 favorite stories / Jan Godfrey ; illustrated by Paola Bertolini Grudina.
    p. cm.
  Includes index.
  ISBN 978-1-4143-2671-9 (hc)
  1. Bible stories, English. I. Grudina, Paola Bertolini. II. Title.
  BS551.3.G63 2009
  220.9'505--dc22   2009008383

Printed and bound in Singapore

13   12   11   10   09
5   4   3   2   1

my story BIBLE
66 Favorite Stories

Jan Godfrey and Paola Bertolini Grudina

TYNDALE KIDS

Tyndale House Publishers, Inc. • Carol Stream, Illinois

C O N T

God Made the World
8

Noah Builds a Boat
10

Under the Stars
12

Three Visitors
14

Isaac and Rebekah
16

Joseph and His Brothers
18

Dreams Come True
20

Little Baby Moses
22

The King Who Said No
24

Follow the Leader
26

The Best Way to Live
28

Joshua's Big Battle
30

God Chooses Gideon
32

Ruth and Naomi
34

The Voice in the Night
36

Seven Sons and a
Shepherd Boy
38

David and Goliath
40

David the Songwriter
42

Solomon
44

Elijah and the Ravens
46

Fire on the Mountain
48

A Dip in the River
50

Jonah Runs the Other Way
52

The Sound of Music
54

Plots and Plans and Lions
56

The Promise of a King
58

A Visitor for Mary
60

A Ride to Bethlehem
62

The Shepherds' Surprise
64

Follow the Star
66

Jesus Gets Lost
68

Jesus Is Baptized
70

Jesus' Prayer
72

E N T S

God Cares about You
74

Very Special Friends
76

Miracle at the Wedding
78

The Hole in the Roof
80

The Story of Two Houses
82

The House That Fell Down
84

The Storm at Sea
86

Little Miss Jairus
88

The Enormous Picnic
90

The Story of the Kind
Stranger
92

Trouble in the Kitchen
94

The Story of the Lost Sheep
96

The Loving Father
98

The Man Who Couldn't See
100

Help Me!
102

The Man Who Climbed
a Tree
104

Jesus Rides a Donkey
106

Less but More
108

A Lonely Garden
110

Three Crosses
112

A Sad Garden
114

A Happy Garden
116

Two Friends along the Road
118

Jesus and Thomas
120

Breakfast on the Shore
122

Jesus Goes to Heaven
124

Wind and Fire
126

Power for the Church
128

A New Follower of Jesus
130

Peter in Prison
132

Shipwreck!
134

Paul Writes Some Letters
136

No More Tears
138

Index of Bible Stories: 140

God Made the World

Long, long, ago, at the beginning of time, God said, "Let there be light," and bright, shining light shone in the darkness.

God said, "Let there be land and sea." So he made wide land and tall mountains and deep water in the sea.

God said, "Let there be trees and plants, sun, moon, and stars." And so the plants produced juicy fruits in the hot sunshine. At night they were cool under the silver moon and twinkly stars.

God said, "Let there be fish and all sorts of winged creatures." So the sea swam with fish, and the sky was filled with birds and butterflies.

God said, "Let there be all kinds of animals." And so snakes slithered and giraffes galloped over the land. Monkeys swung through the trees, and

8

hippos bathed in the rivers.

God said, "Now let there be people to look after my beautiful world." And there were.

God looked at his wonderful creation and saw that it was good. Then he rested. GENESIS 1–2

Noah Builds a Boat

God told Noah it was going to rain very hard. So Noah built a boat. Hammer, hammer, bang, bang! It was a very, very big boat called an ark. God told Noah to take his family and two of each kind of animal into the ark. Plod, plod, clip, clop! They went

into the ark, two by two by two by two by two.

Once God had closed the door of the ark, the rain started to fall. Splish, splash, splosh, splush!

The water covered the ground. The water covered the trees. The water covered the

mountaintops. But the ark bobbed along on the waves, with Noah and the animals safe inside. Days and days and days passed before the rain stopped raining.

Noah opened a window to let a dove fly out. Flap, flap, coo, coo! Then at last the dove came back with a leaf in its beak.

After the water went down, God told Noah it was safe for his family and the animals to come out of the ark. Then God sent a beautiful rainbow.

"There will never be a flood like this again," God promised.

GENESIS 6–9

Under the Stars

A very long time ago, a man named Abram (who later became Abraham) lived in a big city called Ur.

God told Abraham to leave Ur. Abraham was to go from place to place, living in a tent, until God gave him a new home.

Abraham trusted God. He knew it would be a difficult journey. Abraham and his wife, Sarah, traveled across dry, rocky hills. It was hard for both of them. It was hard for their servants and their sheep and goats.

"Come and look at the stars," God said to Abraham one dark and twinkly night. "You are just the beginning. There will be many, many people in your family. There will be many, many children born to the people in your family. There will be many—just like the stars you see in the sky."

Abraham was confused. He and Sarah had no children, and they were getting old. How could this be?

But Abraham knew God. He knew that God always keeps his promises. GENESIS 12:1-8; 15

Three Visitors

One sunny day, three visitors came to Abraham as he sat in the shade near his tent.

This was a surprise. It was very hot for traveling.

"Here's water for washing and drinking," said Abraham. Then he served them a meal that Sarah cooked for them. They ate bread and meat and yogurt and milk under the cool trees.

Sarah stayed in the tent. She hid there and listened to the men talking.

"You will have a child quite soon," said one of the men to Abraham. "Sarah will give birth to a baby boy."

Sarah laughed. "I'm much too old to have a baby! I'm old enough to be a grandma!"

"Why did you laugh?" asked the visitor.

"I didn't—not really," said Sarah, feeling rather silly.

"Oh, yes, you did!" said the visitor. "But nothing is too hard for God to do. You wait and see."

Then Abraham knew that the visitors were like angels from God and that he and Sarah would have a son.

So they did wait, and they did see, because one day quite soon after that, Sarah's baby boy was born. His name was Isaac. GENESIS 18:1-15; 21:1-7

Isaac and Rebekah

When Isaac was grown up, his father, Abraham, wanted to find a good wife for him to marry. So he sent his servant on a journey back to his homeland to find one. The servant took ten camels with him.

When he stopped by a well, the servant asked God to send a girl who would bring water for him—and for his ten thirsty camels! A girl like that would be a good wife for Isaac.

The servant watched as a beautiful girl named Rebekah came to speak to him.

"Would you like some water?" she asked him. "Can I give your camels water too?"

Rebekah was very surprised when the servant gave her two gold bracelets! The servant met her family and found out they were related to Abraham. He gave them presents as well. He knew that God had sent him to the right place.

Then he took Rebekah on the long journey back with him to Abraham and Isaac.

Isaac was out in the fields when he saw Rebekah and the camels coming toward him in the distance. Soon Isaac married her, and he loved her very much. GENESIS 24

Joseph and His Brothers

Joseph had a beautiful coat. It was a present from his father, Jacob.

Joseph had eleven brothers. They were very jealous of him.

"Not fair, not fair," they grumbled.

Joseph had strange dreams. He dreamed about the sun and the moon and the stars. They bowed down to him! He dreamed about bundles of wheat that his brothers had grown. They all bowed down to Joseph's bundles!

"You think you're special, do you?" muttered his brothers. "You think we'll bow down to you, do you? Ha!"

They were so angry that they threw Joseph into a deep, dark pit. Then they dragged him out and sold him to some traders—just as if he were a goat or a basket of fruit!

They pretended a wild animal had killed him. Joseph's father was very, very sad.

But God looked after Joseph.

Joseph was taken to Egypt, and he became a slave. He worked for a kind master, but then he was unfairly put in prison. And then . . . he was taken to see the king of Egypt! GENESIS 37; 39–41:14

Dreams Come True

The king of Egypt had strange dreams, and he was told that Joseph could help him.

"I saw seven thin, skinny cows eat up seven plump, fat cows!" said the king. Moo, moo, moo, moo, moo, moo, moo! Moo, moo, moo, moo, moo, moo, moo. "Then I saw seven dried-up stalks of wheat eat up seven healthy stalks of wheat!"

"It means there will be seven years when there will be plenty to eat," said Joseph. "Then there will be seven years when there will be nothing to eat at all!"

Then Joseph became an important person in Egypt, almost as important as the king himself. He helped people save up lots and lots and lots of food.

The people of Egypt did not go hungry, but everyone in Joseph's family in Canaan was very hungry. Soon Joseph's brothers came to buy food. They bowed low before Joseph, but they didn't know who he was.

Joseph remembered how jealous they had been of him. Joseph remembered the horrible things they had done to him. Joseph remembered the dream he'd had when the sun and moon and stars bowed down to him—and he knew that God had made everything good again.

"I am your brother," said Joseph. "Bring our father here so we can all be together again—and we will all have plenty to eat!" GENESIS 41–47

Little Baby Moses

"Waahhh!" cried little baby Moses. "Waahhh!"

Moses' mom was terribly afraid that the king or his soldiers would hear him crying. And as he grew bigger, his tears grew bigger and he cried even more loudly.

"WAAHHH!"

"WAAHHH!"

"WAAHHH!"

"Oh dear," said Moses' mom. "I wish you wouldn't cry so loudly. The king doesn't like baby boys one bit. He doesn't like baby boys at all, because they will grow up into men who might fight him. We can't let him hear you. He might get so angry that he will kill you!"

Then Moses' mom had a very good idea. She made a basket out of straw and sticky tar that would float safely on the water. Then she laid baby Moses inside.

"Go and watch," said Moses' mom to Moses' big sister, Miriam.

Miriam hid by the river and watched her baby brother bobbing along in the basket. First he giggled and cooed.

Then he cried. "WAAHHH!"

And who should come along but the king's own daughter!

"Oh!" said the princess. "A baby! I'll take care of you, little baby."

"I'll find a nanny to help you," said Miriam. And she brought her own mom, baby Moses' mom!

Now everyone was happy. And God had kept baby Moses safe. EXODUS 2:1-10

The King Who Said No

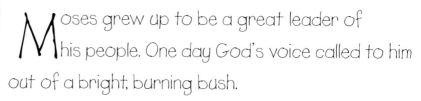

Moses grew up to be a great leader of his people. One day God's voice called to him out of a bright, burning bush.

"Moses, you are going to lead my people out of Egypt to a better country," said God.

"Oh, no, I'm not," said Moses fearfully. He shivered in his shoes.

"Oh, yes, you are," said God firmly. "And take off those shoes. This ground you are standing on is holy and special. You are going to make the king of Egypt let my people go. But I promise I will help you."

"Okay, God," said Moses with a sigh. "I'll do as you ask."

After that, all sorts of things happened.

"Let my people go," said Moses to the king of Egypt. But the king of Egypt wouldn't listen.

So . . . the rivers turned red. Yuck! There was no fresh water.

There were frogs and gnats and flies everywhere, hopping and humming and buzzing.

Animals and people got sick.

Huge hailstones rained down from the dark sky.

Clouds of insects came, chewing and chomping at the crops until the ground was bare.

"Let my people go!" said Moses to the king. But still the king said, "No!"

Finally, when every firstborn son and animal in Egypt died, Moses led his people away from Egypt. EXODUS 3–12

Follow the Leader

Every day a tall cloud showed Moses and the people where to go. Every night a tall fire gave them light and showed them where to rest. When they reached the Red Sea, Moses lifted his special wooden stick and the wind started blowing. The water flowed to each side, and everyone went across.

God provided food called manna when the people were hungry. It appeared on the ground early in the morning and tasted sweet, like honey.

God provided water when they were thirsty. Moses touched a rock with his special wooden stick,

and water flowed out. But still, not everyone was happy. The people grumbled day by day. The people followed Moses day by day. And Moses followed God day by day.

One day Moses talked with God high on a mountain. Thunder rumbled and clouds covered the mountain. The people were afraid. But when Moses came down from the mountain, he brought them God's rules—ten special rules to help them follow God and be happy.

EXODUS 13:17–17:7; 19–20

27

The Best Way to Live

God gave Moses ten special rules written on two big stones. The rules were to make us and other people happy and to help us live good lives.

"I am the true and living God," said God. "Don't worship anyone else except me.

"Don't worship pictures or statues. I am much greater than any beautiful picture or statue.

"And don't use my name wrongly," said God. "My name is special and holy. Treat it with respect.

"The seventh day of the week is special," said God. "It's a rest day, a family day, a happy day, a holy day. It's a day when everyone can worship me together. Even the animals can have a rest!

"Treat your moms and dads well," said God. "Be polite and loving and respectful and kind and obedient to them.

"And don't hurt anyone or even think about hurting them. Don't kill anyone.

"Don't take someone else's wife or husband and treat that person like your own wife or husband.

"Don't steal from people or take anything that belongs to them without asking first.

"And don't tell lies or say mean things about other people.

"Don't look at the things other people have and want them so much that you can't think about anything else."

"There you go," said Moses to the people. "This is what God has said. This is the best way to live."

EXODUS 20:1-21

Joshua's Big Battle

When Moses died, Joshua led the people. God told Joshua to be brave and to trust him, because he was going to take Joshua and his people into the land where he'd promised they would live.

First they had to cross the Jordan River, which was wide and fast and deep and dangerous.

"The living God is with us," Joshua told the people. "Don't be afraid!"

As the priests stepped into the river, it dried up! Everyone was able to cross safely and make their way toward the city of Jericho.

Then they had to get past the city walls, which were tall and thick and high and wide.

"God will give us the city," said Joshua. "Don't be afraid!"

Joshua sent his soldiers to march around the city walls—one, two, three, four, five, six, and seven times. The priests blew their trumpets—very noisily and very loudly—and everybody shouted! Then . . . CRASH! The walls of the city fell down!

Joshua and God's people won the battle of Jericho and were able to live in Canaan, the land that God had promised them. JOSHUA 1; 3; 6

God Chooses Gideon

Gideon was a good man, but he was afraid of his enemies. The Midianites came on their camels and took all the food that God's people were growing. Gideon hid so they would not find him. Then God sent an angel to visit him.

"Hello, you strong, brave man!" said the angel. "God wants you to help his people."

Gideon looked around to see who the angel could be talking to. Surely it was someone else!

"People have stopped worshiping God. That's why your enemies are taking your food and making your lives difficult. God wants you to protect his people from them."

"But I am no one! I am not big or smart or special, and my family is not big or smart or special. If God really wants me to help, I need him to show me he really means me!"

God heard Gideon. One day he made Gideon's piece of wool

wet with dew when the ground around it was dry. Another day he made Gideon's piece of wool dry when the ground was wet.

Then Gideon knew that God had chosen him to help his people. He trusted God and did all that God told him. The Midianites were driven away, and the Israelites could live in safety again.

JUDGES 6–7; 8:28

Ruth and Naomi

Ruth was kind and good. Naomi was sad, because many people in her family had died.

Ruth went to Naomi's faraway country with her so Naomi

34

would not be alone. For Ruth, the country was strange. The country was new.

"You're like my own mother," said Ruth. "I will stay with you and your people in your country, and I will worship the same true God."

Ruth worked in the field so there would be food for them both. Boaz, who owned the field, was kind and good. He offered to take care of Ruth and made sure she had enough food to take home to Naomi.

"God is so kind and good to us!" said Naomi. "He has sent us here to Boaz, who is one of our own family!"

Boaz could see that Ruth was kind and good. He wanted to marry her. He made sure no one else would mind. And he made sure Ruth would be happy to marry him. Then Boaz married Ruth, and they were very happy together. They had a baby boy named Obed.

Naomi wasn't sad anymore. She was happy to have Ruth in her family and to hold her little grandchild. RUTH 1-4

The Voice in the Night

Long, long ago there lived a lady named Hannah. She wanted a baby of her very own.

"Please help me," Hannah prayed to God. "I want a baby so much, and any child I have will be yours as well."

At last, God gave Hannah a baby boy, and she took him to the temple. She was very, very happy.

"Thank you, God," said Hannah.

"I will take care of Samuel," said the priest Eli. "I'll teach him about God. I'll teach him the right way to live. I'll be kind to him."

One night Samuel was sleeping when he heard someone calling his name.

"Samuel!"

Samuel ran to Eli.

"Here I am," said Samuel.

"I didn't call you," said Eli. "Go back to bed."

Then Samuel heard someone calling his name—again.

"Samuel!"

Once . . . twice. . . . Samuel ran to Eli—again.

"Here I am," said Samuel—again.

"I didn't call you," said Eli—again. "Go back to bed."

So Samuel went back to bed—again.

Then he heard his name being called once more.

"Samuel!"

Once . . . twice . . . three times.

This time Eli knew it was God calling Samuel.

"Tell God you're listening to him," said Eli.

"I'm listening, God," said Samuel. "I will always listen to you." 1 SAMUEL 1; 3:1-14

Seven Sons and a Shepherd Boy

Who would be the next king? Samuel, who was now all grown up, asked God to help him choose the right person.

At a special ceremony, a man named Jesse brought seven of his sons to Samuel. They stood before Samuel one by one.

Should it be the tallest and the strongest? thought Samuel. One … two … three … four … five … six … seven. All of them were tall and strong.

Then God whispered in Samuel's ear, "Not the tallest, not the strongest. Only the person who's good and true inside is the one I have chosen to be the king."

Samuel thought hard. "Do you have any other sons?"

"Well, there's David," said Jesse. "But he's only a young boy, a shepherd boy. He's out in the fields with the sheep right now."

"I'll wait," said Samuel. "Send him to me."

David came in from the fields, healthy and happy. Samuel looked him up and down.

"This is the one God has chosen to be king," said Samuel. "Not the tallest, not the strongest, but the person who's good and true inside."

He sprinkled a few drops of oil on David's head as his brothers watched. David knew that God would always be there to help him.

1 SAMUEL 16:1-13

David and Goliath

David, the shepherd boy, was not very big. The enemy, Goliath, was very, very large. He was huge. He was enormous. He was vast.

He was ginormous. He was a GIANT!

Goliath's army stood on one side smiling. King Saul's army stood on the other side looking very worried.

Goliath marched boldly toward King Saul's army. He was wearing a lot of heavy armor. He looked very mean and fierce and full of badness. Everyone was very, very afraid of him.

"I'll go out and fight him," said David. "God helped me fight lions and bears when I took care of my sheep. He will help me now."

King Saul let David wear his heavy armor. But the armor was so heavy he could hardly move. David took it off again and

went to face Goliath.

"YOU?!" roared the giant.
"Who are YOU?!"

David had five stones in his
bag. One ... two ... three
... four ... five. He
whirled one around
in his sling. Then ...
WHAM! Goliath
fell to the ground.
And that was the
end of Goliath—the
big, bold giant who was
full of badness. King Saul's
army cheered and shouted.
Goliath's army turned and
ran away! 1 SAMUEL 17

David the Songwriter

King David wrote a lot of songs. Some of his songs were happy, and some were sad. Some were quiet, and some were bold. Some were praises, and some were prayers.

King David wrote songs about God. These were special songs, called psalms. In some, David sang about how great God is. In others, David asked God to help him. David told God everything, because God was David's friend.

David knew that God was always with him when he felt happy and sang and danced and shouted for joy. He knew that God was always with him when he felt sad and frightened and lonely and grumpy.

One of the songs he wrote was about God being like a good shepherd.

The Lord's my shepherd, and I'm his sheep.
He leads me where it's rough and steep
or by still waters, cool and deep.
He walks beside me every day,
in all the places where I play,
in every step along the way.

42

I walk behind him in his light,

in the darkness shining bright.

I know I'm always in his sight.

He spreads out food and comes to greet:

"Everybody, take a seat!

Everybody, come and eat!" PSALM 23

43

Solomon

King Solomon had a dream one night.

"What would you like me to give you?" asked God.

Solomon thought hard. Did he want to be rich and great and have lots of money? Did he want to be famous and strong and brave? Did he want lots of wonderful things for himself?

Then Solomon answered God. "I think really I'd like to be good and wise, fair and just and true—a really good and obedient king. I'd like to rule my people well."

"Good," said God. "Excellent. That's great. You will be a good and wise king, and I'll give you a lot more besides."

So King Solomon was a good and wise king. All sorts of people came to him. He told them things that were good and true and helpful. He taught them how to live wise and happy lives.

Then King Solomon built a great and wonderful Temple for God. It was made of gold and bronze and wood and stones, with many, many beautifully carved decorations.

"This Temple building is a place for your people to come and pray to you and tell you how great you are," Solomon said to God. "But I know that you are with us, God, wherever we are."

1 KINGS 3; 5-8

Elijah and the Ravens

I t's not going to rain for a very long time," said the prophet Elijah to King Ahab. "God has said so. He's not at all happy with the bad things you have been doing.

"There won't be much to eat. There won't be much to drink. Nothing will grow, and the earth will be dry and bare."

"Hmmm," said King Ahab, who wasn't sure whether to believe Elijah or not.

Then God told Elijah to go and stay by a little stream. "You can drink the water there, and I will send birds to feed you."

Elijah drank from the little stream. Every morning and every evening, birds came to Elijah—large black ravens—and they brought him food to eat. Then just as God had said, it stopped raining, and soon Elijah's little stream dried up.

"Now go to the little village of Zarephath," God told Elijah. "There is a woman there who will make sure you have enough to eat."

"It's all I have left," the woman told Elijah. "After this I have no more flour or oil to make bread."

But for as long as she shared the woman food with Elijah, God made sure that the little jar of flour and the little bottle of oil did not run out. 1 KINGS 17

47

Fire on the Mountain

There was still no rain. It was time for Elijah to go back to the king.

"What's going on?" grumbled King Ahab.

"Let's choose between the real God and the stone statue you call Baal," said Elijah. "We'll soon see who will set fire to the altar and send rain again—the true and living God or a fake god made of stone named Baal."

Elijah laid out wood on top of stones, ready for God to bring a fire. And the people who believed Baal was god laid out wood on top of stones, ready for Baal to bring a fire.

"Come on, Baal!" shouted the people who worshiped the pretend god. "Light the fire! Listen to us

and answer! Listen to us! LISTEN TO US!"

They shouted and danced until they were exhausted and their throats were sore. But nothing happened.

"Has Baal run away?" teased Elijah. "Perhaps he's asleep! Or maybe he's on vacation!"

Elijah poured water all around his stones. Then he talked to God. "Let everyone see that you are the one true and living God," prayed Elijah.

Suddenly there was fire from heaven. The wood sizzled. The fire sizzled. Then God sent the rain, like only the real God could! 1 KINGS 18

A Dip in the River

Naaman was an important soldier, but he had spots and blotches and sore places all over his skin. A little servant girl lived with Naaman and his wife. She wanted to help.

"There's a man in my country who can make Naaman well again," said the girl. "His name is Elisha. He is a prophet from God."

So Naaman sent a message to the king of the servant girl's country.

"No good asking me," the king said. "I can't make you better. But you could go and visit Elisha."

So Naaman went to visit Elisha.

"Go and wash in the Jordan River seven times," said Elisha's servant.

Naaman wasn't very happy. "First he sends his servant instead of seeing me himself. Then he tells me to take a bath! I thought he'd do something special—wave his arms or say some prayers or make me well right away! Grrrr!"

"Go on, Naaman," said his friends. "Just do it!"

"Oh all right," said Naaman. Grumpily, he went to the river. In he went. Dip, dip, dip, dip, dip, dip, dip. . . .

And the spots and blotches vanished!

"Wow!" said Naaman. "Now I know that God is real. Thank you, God! You really are special!" 2 KINGS 5:1-19

51

Jonah Runs the Other Way

God told Jonah to go to a city called Nineveh.

"The people there do a lot of wrong things," said God. "I want you to tell them about me."

But Jonah didn't want to go to Nineveh. So he tried to run away from God and sailed to another place instead. A big storm blew, and the sailors were afraid they would all drown.

"Throw me into the sea!" said Jonah. "It's all my fault! I've disobeyed God."

"Okay," said the sailors. "If that's what you want."

As soon as Jonah was tossed overboard, the sea became calm.

Then . . . gulp, swallow, gulp!

An enormous big fish swallowed Jonah.

It was rather dark inside.

Jonah stayed there for three days and three nights. He prayed to God.

Then . . . gulp, guggle, whoosh!

The enormous big fish tossed

Jonah out of its mouth and onto the beach. This time Jonah did as God had told him. He went to the city of Nineveh. He told the people there that they had done wrong things and that they needed to follow God.

Then the people said they were sorry, and God saved them.

"I'm glad these people are sorry for doing wrong things and not following me," said God. JONAH 1–3

The Sound of Music

Three friends were taken as prisoners to a place called Babylon, far away from home. They worshiped the one true God, but the king worshiped pretend gods.

One day the king told everyone to bow down and worship a golden statue.

"I won't," said Shadrach.

"I won't," said his friend Meshach.

"I won't," said his friend Abednego.

"There will be trouble if you don't!" said a messenger of the king.

"As soon as you hear music and instruments, you'll bow down to that golden statue, or there'll be trouble—you wait and see! If you don't bow down and worship it, you'll be thrown into a fiery furnace!"

The three friends still would not worship the golden statue.

"We will only worship the one true God," they said.

So they were thrown into the blazing, fiery furnace. It was very, very, very hot.

But they did not die. They did not get burned. They didn't even smell smoky! God sent an angel into the fiery furnace to keep them safe. When the king brought them out of the fiery furnace, he knew that their God was the one true God! DANIEL 1, 3

Plots and Plans and Lions

The king's men didn't like Daniel because he was good and wise. They were jealous of him.

So they planned and plotted, they muttered and mumbled, they whispered and whined, and they schemed skillfully, with their heads bent close together.

"Anyone who doesn't treat you like a god, oh King, will be thrown to the lions," they said, bowing low.

"Okay!" said the king.

Daniel prayed to God every day at his open window.

The king's men saw him, and they told the king.

"Daniel prays to God instead of to you," they said.

"Daniel likes God best," they said.

"Daniel doesn't worship you as he should," they said.

"Daniel—"

"Shh!" said the king. "Enough!" The king wasn't very happy about throwing Daniel to the lions, but he had to do as he'd agreed.

"I hope your God will save you," he said to Daniel as he sent him to the lions' den.

"GGGGGGGGGGGRRRRRRRRRRRR!"

The lions were hungry . . . and it was a long, lonely night for the king.

In the morning the king found Daniel . . . alive and well!

The lions were walking around quietly.

"God took care of me," said Daniel. "I trusted him."

"Daniel's God is a living God," said the king in amazement. "He will rule forever!" DANIEL 6

The Promise of a King

"One day," said God, "the darkness and shadows will disappear. There will be peace and joy and light and a Kingdom of sunshine and happiness.

"A child will be born to you, a very special child. A son will be given to you, a very special son. There will be a Kingdom of peace, where wild animals and children will rest together.

"Everyone," continued God, "will know about love and truth and peace and joy. For

a wonderful King is coming. Meanwhile . . . just wait. Just wait and see, and trust in me!" ISAIAH 9:1-7; 11:1-9; 55:12-13

A Visitor for Mary

One day a girl named Mary had a big surprise.

Mary was all by herself when an angel came to her. The angel's name was Gabriel.

"Don't be afraid," said the angel Gabriel gently. "I have a message for you from God. You are going to have a baby. The baby will be named Jesus, and he will be the Son of God."

Mary was afraid, but she was also very happy.

She hurried to tell her cousin Elizabeth, and they praised God together.

"I'm so happy," Mary sang to God. "You're wise and wonderful! You're the greatest and the best!" LUKE 1:26-55

A Ride to Bethlehem

It was nearly time for Mary's baby to be born. But Mary and Joseph had to travel a long way to Bethlehem.

When they reached the town, there were lots of visitors. There was nowhere for them to stay.

"No room!" said one innkeeper.

"No room!" said another.

"No room!" said one more.

All the inns were full of people. All the streets were full of people. All the town was full of people.

At last one of the innkeepers

felt sorry for Mary and Joseph. He saw how tired they were. He could see that Mary's baby would soon be born.

"You can rest in the stable," he said. And that night Mary's baby was born. He was Jesus, the Son of God.

Mary wrapped him in cloth and made a bed for him in the manger, the place where the animals ate. LUKE 2:1-7

63

The Shepherds' Surprise

The night Jesus was born, shepherds were out in the fields taking care of their sheep. It was cold and quiet and dark ... until suddenly there was a bright light all around them! An angel with them!

"Don't be afraid," said the angel. "I have good news for you. Jesus, the Son of God, has been born in Bethlehem. You'll find him lying in a manger."

Then lots more angels appeared—a sky full of angels!

"Glory to God!" they sang.

The shepherds rubbed their eyes in surprise. The sky grew dark again. What was happening? They ran to Bethlehem to see if it could be true—and there was the baby in the manger.

"Guess what happened?" said the shepherds to Mary and Joseph. "There were angels . . . and listen to what they said about this baby!"

With Joseph at her side, Mary thought hard about the angels' message and the special baby lying in the manger. The shepherds went back to their sheep, praising God because his own Son had been born—and they had seen him! *LUKE 2:8-20*

Follow the Star

A very bright star shone high in the sky.

Some wise men, who knew a lot about the stars, followed the bright star. They knew it was a sign from God, a sign that would lead them to the newborn King.

They made a long, long journey, following the bright star all the way, to find the newborn King.

"We will bring him gifts just right for a king," they said.

"I will bring him gold," said one.

"I will bring him frankincense," said another.

"I will bring him myrrh," said a third.

They traveled on and on . . . and on . . . and on . . . all the time following the bright star, until at last the wise men found Jesus with Mary, his mother. They knelt down in awe and gave him their gifts of gold, frankincense, and myrrh. They worshiped Jesus, the Son of God.

Then the wise men traveled home again to their lands in the East. MATTHEW 2:1-12

Jesus Gets Lost

Jesus was growing up. Every year he went to the Temple in Jerusalem with his mother, Mary, and Joseph, for a special celebration called the Passover.

When Jesus was twelve years old, his parents got very worried when they couldn't find him.

As usual, there were crowds of people in Jerusalem. As usual, Mary and Joseph left Jerusalem with everyone else.

After a while, Mary said, "Where's Jesus?"

"I think he's with those people over there," said Joseph, looking. But they couldn't find Jesus anywhere!

"Jesus, where are you?" called Mary and Joseph. They shouted his name and asked people and looked everywhere, but they still couldn't find Jesus! So Mary and Joseph went back to Jerusalem.

They found him in the Temple listening to the teachers. "Where have you been?" asked Mary anxiously.

"We've been very worried!" said

Joseph. "We've been looking all over for you."

"I was just fine," said Jesus. "You shouldn't have wondered where I was. I needed to be in God's house—my Father's house—so I could learn all about him."

Jesus went back home with Mary and Joseph. He grew taller and stronger, and he kept on learning about God. LUKE 2:41-52

Jesus Is Baptized

A man named John lived in the desert. He wore rough, scratchy clothes, and he ate insects and honey.

John told people that a very special person, Jesus, the Messiah, was coming.

"Get ready for him, get ready!" said John. "God is sending us a King. You need to be sorry for all the wrong things you've ever done. And you need to be baptized as a sign that God is washing you clean."

Then one day Jesus himself came and asked John to baptize him in the Jordan River.

John was surprised. He realized that Jesus was the special King God had promised. John believed that Jesus was the Messiah. John knew that Jesus was the Son of God.

John did as Jesus asked. He baptized him.

As Jesus came up out of the water, John saw a dove fluttering around above Jesus' head.

He heard God's voice speaking from heaven. "This is my Son," said God. "I am very happy with him." MATTHEW 3

Jesus' Prayer

Jesus told people how to pray to God.

"God loves to hear his children pray to him," said Jesus. "But you don't have to use long words that don't mean much. Be honest with God. Tell him how you really feel."

Then Jesus gave them an example to use to help them. Some people call this the Lord's Prayer.

Our Father in heaven, your name is great and holy.
We want to do what is right so that your love will spread all
over the world.
Please give everyone enough to eat each day, and help us to
be kind to each other always.
Keep us safe from harm and from doing wrong things.

For you are true and wonderful and glorious, and your
Kingdom will last forever and ever and ever.
Amen. MATTHEW 6:5-13

God Cares about You

"Don't worry too much about your food and drink and clothes," said Jesus.

"Look at the birds and the flowers. Our heavenly Father God takes care of the birds, and they all find food.

"And look how the wildflowers grow. God has made them look beautiful. They're as nice and colorful as a king's clothes.

"God gives us all we need when we love him and trust him and share with each other. Then there will be enough food and drink and clothes for everyone."

Later Jesus watched some sparrows as the tiny birds flew and hopped around and pecked at the ground.

"God knows and cares for everyone, even the tiniest of these sparrows," said Jesus. "God is great and mighty and powerful, but he knows every little bird. A little sparrow doesn't seem very important, but God knows if one falls to the ground. He knows us and cares for each one of us, too. We don't need to be afraid when we know we're safe in his strong, kind hands."

MATTHEW 6:25-33; 10:29-31

Very Special Friends

Jesus decided to choose twelve very special friends. He wanted them to go everywhere with him and help him in his work of telling people all about God, making sick people feel better, making bad people want to be good, and making sad people happy and smiley again.

Jesus called to four fishermen— Peter, Andrew, James, and John. They were busy with their nets beside the sea.

"Hello there!" called Jesus. "Leave your nets, and come follow me!" And they did.

Later on, Jesus met Matthew. No one liked him much. He sat counting his money.

"Hello there!" said Jesus. "Leave your money, and come follow me!" And Matthew did.

Jesus asked God to help him choose the right people to be his friends. Here they all are: Peter, Andrew, James, John, Philip, Bartholomew, Matthew, Thomas, James (yes, there were two!), Thaddaeus, Simon, and Judas.

Can you count them?

Altogether there were twelve very special friends.

Sometimes they went out two by two, telling everyone some very good news.

"God loves you!" they said. "God is great!

"God wants you to love him and follow him.

"God wants you to love other people and to be part of his special Kingdom."

MATTHEW 4:18-22; 9:9; 10:1-8

Miracle at the Wedding

Jesus went with his mother, Mary, and his friends to a wedding. It was a happy time, with talking and laughing, family and friends and fun. There were lots of good things to eat and drink . . . until suddenly there was no wine left. It had all run out! There was nothing left for the guests to drink.

Mary spoke to Jesus. "There's no wine left. Please do something! Please help, or the party will be ruined for everyone!"

"Fill the jars with water," Jesus said to the servants. "Fill them right up to the top, then take it to the guests."

The servants did exactly what Jesus told them, and then
something amazing happened. As it was poured, the water turned
into the best wine of all.

Jesus' friends watched in awe. Their eyes opened wider and
wider. So did the eyes of the host at the wedding party when he
tasted the wine.

"My goodness!" he said. "What a surprise! I can't believe you
kept this wine until now. It's wonderful! It's the best!"

Jesus' disciples were amazed.

"Jesus is wonderful and special," they said. "He can do anything!"

JOHN 2:1-11

The Hole in the Roof

Jesus was in town!

And so was a man who couldn't walk. He lay on a mattress until his four kind friends carried him to Jesus.

But they found a huge crowd of people filling the house where

Jesus was. They couldn't get inside the house. They couldn't see Jesus at all!

Then the four friends had a good idea. They climbed up and carried their friend onto the top of the house.

They scratched and scraped at the roof until they had made a little hole. Parts of the roof fell and flew everywhere until the hole grew bigger . . . and bigger . . . until it was so big they could let their friend down into the house–right at Jesus' feet.

"Well, hello there," said Jesus.

Jesus told the man he would forgive him for anything he'd ever done wrong. Some of the people started complaining.

"Who does Jesus think he is?" they muttered.

Others were surprised. All were amazed!

Then Jesus said to the man, "Pick up your mattress and walk home."

And he did!

"We've never seen anything like this!" said all the people. And they praised God. LUKE 5:17-26

The Story of Two Houses

Jesus told a story about two men and two houses.

"I think I'll build a house," said the first man, who was sensible and wise. "I'll build it over there on that big, strong rock. That rock looks good and solid and safe. It will be the perfect place for a house."

The first man's house was a very fine house when it was finished. Its little windows looked out at the rock it was built on—good and solid and safe. It was a very fine house indeed.

"I'm going to build a house too," said the second man, who was foolish and silly. "But I'm going to build mine over there on the sand. Rocks are dull and boring. My house will be on a beautiful, wide golden beach."

The second man's house was a very fine house when it was finished. Its little windows looked out at the sand it was built on—a beautiful, wide golden beach. It was a very fine house indeed.

But soon a storm came. . . . LUKE 6:47-49

The House That Fell Down

One day there was a great storm. The rain rained—pitter-patter. The rivers rose—higher and higher. The wind whistled. Whoooooooo!

The first man sat in his fine house and heard the big storm rumble and clatter and blow around him.

"I'm surrounded by a slushy, sloshing storm!" he said. "The wind is rustling, the rain is dripping and drowning, and the trees are shaking. But I'm standing firm and dry, safe and sound on my strong foundation! My house is built on the hard and solid rock!"

The second man sat in his fine house and heard the great storm rumble and clatter and blow around him.

"The wind is coming in my windows, my walls are weak and

wobbling, my floors are falling in, my upstairs is downstairs, and my stones are sliding into the slippery sand! Ohhhhhhhhhhhhhhhh!"

"Which is wiser?" asked Jesus. "To build on a rock or to build on sand? Listen closely to this story. Make sure your life is built on the solid rock of my words, which are true and strong. They will not tumble around you when troubles come." LUKE 6:47-49

The Storm at Sea

Jesus and his friends were out in a boat on the lake. Everything was very quiet and still.

Soon Jesus fell asleep. It had been a long day, and he was very tired.

Then—suddenly—there was a big storm!

The wind blew. Whoooooooooooooooo!

The waves crashed. Splash! Wisshh! Whoosh!

Some of the waves splashed into the boat. The wind tossed the boat up and down, up and down.

But Jesus stayed fast asleep.

Jesus' friends were very afraid.

"Wake up!" they said to Jesus. "Wake up! WAKE UP!"

Jesus woke up. He stood up. He spoke to the wind.

"Hush...be quiet," said Jesus. And the wind was quiet.

Then Jesus spoke to the waves.

"Hush...calm down," said Jesus. And the waves were calm.

The wind and the waves both did as Jesus said. Everything became calm...and quiet ...and still.

Jesus' friends weren't afraid now. Their wonderful friend Jesus had calmed the storm! LUKE 8:22-25

Little Miss Jairus

Little Miss Jairus was very sick. She lay in bed feeling tired and achy. She was so sick that Jairus, her daddy, went to find Jesus.

"I know he can help us," said Jairus. "Jesus helps everybody."

And that day, it seemed like everybody did want Jesus' help. There were crowds of people everywhere. They pushed and pulled and shouted and shoved and poked and prodded to get near Jesus. So it took Jesus a long time to reach Jairus's house.

Jesus' friends Peter and James and John went with him. When at last they reached the house, everyone was wailing and crying and feeling very sad.

"You're too late, Jesus," they said, sobbing. "She's already dead."

"Stop crying," said Jesus. "She's just asleep."

Then the girl's mom and dad and Peter and James and John watched. Jesus took the girl's hands and said, "Get up, little girl! Wake up. Stand up!"

And Little Miss Jairus did get up. She woke up! She stood up! She was well again!

Jesus said to everyone else, "Cheer up! This girl is hungry! Find her something to eat."

Then Little Miss Jairus and her mom and dad were very, very happy that Jesus had made her well again. LUKE 8:40-42, 49-56

The Enormous Picnic

Lots of people had been listening to Jesus. There were thousands of them on the hillside! They heard him tell stories. They heard him talk about God—and heard that Jesus really knew what God is like. They saw him make blind people see and sick people better. The people followed Jesus anywhere.

By evening everyone was hungry, but—oh dear!—they were too far from home and there was nothing to eat.

Then a little boy came to Jesus with all the food he had. He gave it to Jesus and his friends—just five flat little bread rolls and two little fish that his mother had given him. The boy shared all he had with Jesus.

"Thank you, God, for all you give us," said Jesus, looking up.

Then Jesus' disciples shared the food until everybody had had enough to eat. It was a big and happy picnic.

There were even twelve baskets of food left over. Jesus' friends picked them all up before everyone went home. JOHN 6:1-13

The Story of the Kind Stranger

How can I show God that I love him?" a man once asked Jesus.

"Love God as well as you can, and love the other people in your life too," Jesus replied. Then Jesus told a story so the man would know what he meant.

"There was a man who was walking from one town to another, and he was beaten and robbed. The man lay by the side of the road. He hurt all over. He felt sick and very sad.

"Then the man heard footsteps in the distance coming nearer . . . louder . . . and then going away softly . . . softly . . . on the other side of the road.

"Then the man heard more footsteps in the distance coming nearer . . . louder . . . and then going away softly . . . softly . . . on the other side of the road.

"Then the man heard clippety-clop, clippety-clop—it was a man on a donkey, a man from another country that people didn't like. He was a stranger, an enemy!

"But the stranger bandaged the man's wounds, helped him onto his donkey, and took him to an inn to rest. The kind stranger paid the innkeeper to keep taking care of the man until he was well enough to leave. Although this man was a stranger, he really cared about the hurt man. That's what love is really like." LUKE 10:25-37

Trouble in the Kitchen

Jesus went to Mary and Martha's house for supper.

Mary liked listening to Jesus. She sat quietly by his feet.
He had so many wonderful stories to tell. He had so many

wonderful things to talk about. He had so many wonderful things to teach.

Martha liked listening to Jesus too. But she was busy getting the meal ready. There was so much work to do: cleaning up, cooking and stirring, mashing and mixing, chopping and peeling, whisking and washing. Some things were bubbling and boiling when they shouldn't have been. Some things weren't doing anything at all when they should have been.

Oh dear, oh dear, oh DEAR! thought Martha, growing more and more worried and flustered. This meal would never be ready for Jesus!

"I have all this work to do on my own!" grumbled Martha to Jesus. "Can't you tell Mary to come and help?"

Jesus smiled. "Don't be so worried, Martha," said Jesus kindly. "Just come and sit down with me. The rest can all wait. We'll have supper later when it's all ready." LUKE 10:38-42

The Story of the Lost Sheep

"God loves you like a good shepherd loves his sheep!" Jesus said. Then he told a story.

"Once there was a shepherd who had one hundred sheep. But one of the sheep wandered off. It nibbled on green grass.

"'I'm happy,' said the little sheep. 'Baaa.'

"The sheep wandered off farther. It nibbled on green grass and skipped and ran.

"'I'm so happy,' said the little sheep. 'Baaa.'

"The sheep wandered farther and farther. It nibbled on green grass and skipped and ran over the hills.

"Then the little sheep wandered farther and farther and farther. It grew dark and cold. There wasn't any more green grass, only rocky hills and prickly bushes.

"'I'm sad and lonely,' said the little sheep. 'I want to go home. I'm tired. I'm hungry. I'm lost! Please won't somebody come and find me?'

"And somebody did.

"The shepherd counted his sheep. Ninety-seven . . . ninety-eight . . . ninety-nine. . . . There was one missing! He left his other sheep and raced over the hillside, shouting and searching, climbing and calling . . . until at last he found his little lost sheep and carried it safely in his arms down the steep, rocky path.

"'I'm really happy I've found you,' said the shepherd. 'Let's have a party! Let's celebrate!'" LUKE 15:3-7

The Loving Father

God loves you," said Jesus. "God loves you so much, he waits for you to come back to him and say you're sorry after you've made a mistake. God is like the father in this story.

"The father had two sons. The younger son ran away from

home and took his part of his father's money with him. Suddenly he was rich! He spent and spent and spent his money on all kinds of things—until one day he'd spent it all!

"Now he didn't have any money left. He was poor. He was so poor that he had to go and work very hard on a pig farm. He was so poor that he got very, very hungry. He was so poor that he ate the pigs' food. He was so poor and hungry that he decided to go home to his father.

"His father saw him coming from a long way away. He was overjoyed to see him. He hugged him and kissed him.

"'I'm really sorry,' said the young man to his father. 'I've done everything wrong—against you and my family and God. I've been selfish and greedy and—'

"But his father was already calling to his servants.

"'He has *come* home!' he shouted. 'My son is home again! Bring my best coat and a ring for his finger and shoes for his feet. Let's celebrate! Let's have a feast! Let's have music and dancing! Let the party begin!'" LUKE 15:11-24

99

The Man Who Couldn't See

Bartimaeus was blind. He couldn't see anything at all.

He couldn't see the flowers, although he could smell them.

He couldn't see the trees, although he could hear the wind rustling their leaves and could feel the rough bark of their trunks when he sat in their shade.

He couldn't see the blue sky and white wispy clouds, although he could feel the hot sun and the cool breeze.

He couldn't see the people around him—although he could hear them laughing and shouting and joking and playing.

Because Bartimaeus could not see, he could not work. Because Bartimaeus could not work, he had no money for food! So he sat by the roadside, day after day, calling out to people, begging them for money.

Bartimaeus's eyes were dark and sad. MARK 10:46

Help Me!

One day Bartimaeus heard people coming down the road. He heard the sound of their feet and knew it was a large crowd. He heard the sound of their voices and knew it was a happy crowd. When Bartimaeus found out that Jesus was coming, he called out to him.

"Jesus!" shouted Bartimaeus. "Help me!"

"Sssssssssshhh!" everybody said, shocked.

But Bartimaeus called out again, more loudly this time, "HELP ME!"

"Sssssssssshhh!" everybody said again, even more shocked.

Jesus said, "Tell Bartimaeus to come here."

Kind hands helped him to his feet, and kind hands led him to Jesus.

"I want to see," said Bartimaeus. "Please!"

"Go along and you'll be well," said Jesus gently. "You will see."

Bartimaeus opened his eyes wider . . . and wider . . . and yes! He could see!

He could see the flowers. He could see the trees. He could see the sky and the clouds, and he could see all the people smiling at him. He could see everything!

He could see Jesus, too, so Bartimaeus followed him along the road.

"Thank you, God!" said Bartimaeus.

"Praise God!" said everyone.

MARK 10:47-52

The Man Who Climbed a Tree

Once there was a little man named Zacchaeus. He was very rich and had a lot of money. He had not been a kind man or a good man, and he didn't have many friends. In fact, he didn't really have any friends. People said he was a cheat.

Zacchaeus was very short. He wanted to see Jesus, who was coming down the road. But lots of other people wanted to see Jesus too. And Zacchaeus couldn't see over their heads. Then he had a good idea.

He climbed into the branches of a fig tree and looked down on all the people. He knew Jesus would come soon.

At last, there was Jesus. Jesus looked up and saw Zacchaeus looking down at him!

"Come down," Jesus said to Zacchaeus. "Hurry, because I want to come to your house today."

Zacchaeus slid down through the branches as fast as a grown man could.

He took Jesus to his home for a meal. Soon he was telling Jesus that he was sorry for the wrong things he'd done.

"You're my friend now," Zacchaeus said to Jesus. "I'll give money back to anyone I have cheated, and I'll share what I have left with the poor."

Then Zacchaeus felt very, very happy.

LUKE 19:1-10

Jesus Rides a Donkey

Jesus and his friends were on their way to the big city of Jerusalem.

"There's a young little donkey over in that village," Jesus said to his friends one day. "It has never been ridden before. The owner will understand that I need it. Untie it and bring it to me."

Carefully, Jesus' special friends got the donkey. They put their coats over the donkey's back and helped Jesus climb on.

Jesus rode along the road to Jerusalem. It was all very noisy and exciting. Crowds of people followed him. Lots of men, lots of women, and lots of children followed him.

They threw their coats down on the road in front of him. They laid down palm branches on the road in front of him. They cheered and waved and shouted. They crowded and pushed so they could see Jesus.

"Hooray!" everyone cried out. "Praise God! Hosanna! Praise the one who saves! Praise King Jesus!"

MATTHEW 21:1-19

Less but More

One day Jesus and his friends were at the Temple together.

They watched people coming and going and dropping money into the offering box. Some rich people put a lot of money in. They made sure people were looking as they put lots of money into the box.

Then a poor woman came along. Her husband was dead, and she had very little money. She didn't look to see who was watching. She didn't care what people thought of her at all. She came because she loved God. That was all.

Quietly she dropped two little coins into the box. "Look," said Jesus to his disciples. "This woman has been really generous.

"The rich people gave a lot. But the rich are rich. They still have lots of money left. This woman hardly has enough to eat. She has given everything she has. So even though she gave less money, she has really given far more." LUKE 21:1-4

A Lonely Garden

Jesus had a special meal with his friends. They ate bread and drank wine together. Jesus told them to remember that special night every time they ate bread and drank wine in the future.

Then they went out into a dark, quiet garden.

Jesus prayed to God.

"I will do whatever you want," said Jesus. "But please help me, Father."

Jesus was sad because Judas, one of his special friends, didn't want to be his friend anymore. He was going to help Jesus' enemies take him away. They would be cruel to him and hurt him.

Jesus' friends were tired. They couldn't keep their eyes open a moment longer. They all fell asleep. Jesus felt sad and lonely.

"Wake up!" Jesus said to them. "Look what's happening."

Suddenly, they saw lights and heard noises. Torches were blazing. Swords were clashing. Rough voices shouting.

Then one of Jesus' friends stepped out of the darkness. He came over to Jesus, pretending to be kind. It was Judas.

Then the soldiers knew.

"That's him!" said a voice.

"There he is!" said another voice.

"Get him!" said one.

"Grab him!" said another.

And the soldiers took Jesus away.

MATTHEW 26:17-30, 36-57

Three Crosses

On a lonely hill one day, Jesus was killed. He was hung on a cross between two other crosses.

There were three crosses—one for a thief, one for a robber, and between them, one for Jesus, God's Son. Jesus had never done anything wrong. He had given the blind their sight and given the deaf their hearing. He loved people, helped them, and made them well.

Jesus asked his Father to forgive the people who had put him on the cross.

Then there was an earthquake. There was darkness in the middle of the day. The curtain in the Temple was torn in half.

The sun went down, and Jesus died.

It was the saddest day there had ever, ever been. LUKE 23:32-49

A Sad Garden

Agood man named Joseph and another man Jesus had helped named Nicodemus carried Jesus' body to a cave in a beautiful garden.

Smells of flowers and spices and trees drifted through the dewy evening air. The garden felt sad and quiet and still.

They buried Jesus in a quiet, dark cave. Then they pushed a very big, heavy stone across the doorway.

No one could get in. No one could get out. That was that. Jesus' mother was very sad. Jesus' friend John was very sad too. All Jesus' friends were very, very sad. They thought they would never see Jesus again.

It was the quietest day there had ever, ever been.

MATTHEW 27:57-61;

JOHN 19:38-42

A Happy Garden

Early on Sunday morning, some women who loved Jesus took their sweet-smelling spices to the garden where he was buried.

But when they reached the cave, they found that the big, heavy stone had been rolled away . . . and the tomb was empty!

Two shining angels sat beside the cave.

"Jesus isn't here," said the angels. "Go and tell everyone he is alive again!"

The women were filled with joy! They ran to tell Peter and Jesus' other friends, but no one could understand what had happened.

Peter and John ran to the garden and saw the empty tomb for themselves, but they still did not understand what had happened. Mary Magdalene stayed by the empty cave, crying. She did not understand what had happened either.

"Why are you crying?" asked a voice behind her.

"They've taken Jesus' body away," she said. "Do you know where he is? I need to find him!"

As Mary turned to look at the man, she realized that it was

Jesus! Mary could hardly believe her eyes. She was so, so happy.

The sun rose and the birds sang. Mary ran back to Peter and Jesus' other friends and told them, "Jesus is alive!"

It was the happiest day there had ever, ever been.

LUKE 24:1-12; JOHN 20:1-18

Two Friends along the Road

That very same evening, a man named Cleopas and his friend were walking to Emmaus, a nearby village.

They talked quietly and sadly, because Jesus had died. Suddenly, a stranger joined them.

"Why are you so sad?" asked the stranger.

"We're sad because Jesus has died," said the two friends.

"We thought he would save us, but now he has been killed."

Then they all went on their way together— Cleopas, his friend, and the

stranger. The stranger talked and they listened. He told them wonderful, exciting things about God.

"Come in and have supper with us," said the friends when they reached Emmaus. "It's getting late and dark."

The stranger broke some bread and gave it to them—and suddenly the friends knew who he was. It was Jesus! Then suddenly . . . he wasn't there anymore!

"We knew he was someone special," said Cleopas.

"We felt warm and happy when he talked to us," said Cleopas's friend.

"Quick, quick!" they said. "Let's go and tell the others! Jesus really is alive!" LUKE 24:13-34

Jesus and Thomas

Yes, Jesus really was alive again! One day when his special friends were all together, Jesus slipped into the room, although the door was firmly shut and locked.

"Peace be with you," said Jesus.

The disciples' eyes opened wider and wider. Their mouths opened wider and wider. They were amazed to see Jesus again.

Could it really be Jesus?

"Don't be afraid," said Jesus kindly. "It really is me, your friend. Look at my hands and feet. You can see where I was hurt. Now how about some fish for supper?"

Thomas had not been with the others. He couldn't believe that Jesus was alive again, walking and talking with his friends, and eating fish for supper!

"But it's true," said his friends. "We've seen him. We've spoken to him. Jesus really is alive!"

The next time Jesus slipped into the room, Thomas was there too.

"Peace be with you," said Jesus again. "Look at me," Jesus said to Thomas. "Look at me and touch me. There's no doubt it's me!"

Thomas looked . . . and looked . . . and looked again . . . and then he knew it was Jesus.

"Jesus!" Thomas said happily. "It really is you. You are my Lord."

LUKE 24:35-49; JOHN 20:19-29

Breakfast on the Shore

One night Peter and his friends were out in their boat, fishing on Lake Galilee.

They fished and fished and fished all night, but they didn't catch any fish at all.

Just as the sun was rising, they heard a man's voice from the water's edge.

"Have you caught anything?" called the man.

"No, nothing," they replied gloomily. "Not even the tiniest, teeniest little fish."

"Try again," the man shouted back to them. "Put out your net on the other side of the boat."

"Come on, everyone," said Peter with a sigh. "One more go. Heave ho!"

So the friends heaved and hoed and put out their net on the other side of the boat.

Suddenly the net was full of big fish—so many fish that the friends could hardly pull in the net! Then they knew who the man on the shore must be.

"It's Jesus!" they said.

Peter jumped into the water and swam to the beach. There was Jesus, making breakfast.

The friends dragged in the net, which was full of wiggling, wriggling fish.

"Come and eat," said Jesus.

And they all ate fish and bread together on the beach.

After breakfast, Jesus gave Peter a special job.

"Always follow me," said Jesus. "And take care of all my friends for me." JOHN 21:1-19

Jesus Goes to Heaven

Jesus and his special friends stood talking to each other on a high hillside.

"Is it time for you to show you are the King of all the earth?" his friends asked Jesus.

"Not quite yet," said Jesus kindly. "One day that will happen. But I'm going back to heaven first. I'm going back to God. For now I want you to tell other people all about me. I want you to tell people how they can follow me. I want you to tell other people that the secret of being happy is to love God and be kind to everyone else. I will always be with you to help you."

Then Jesus asked God to bless his friends and love them.

As he spoke, a cloud came down over the hillside. When the cloud moved away, Jesus had vanished.

His friends stared and stared up at the clear sky.

Then two angels stood beside them.

"Don't go on looking at the sky," said the angels. "One day Jesus will come back again, just as he promised." LUKE 24:50-52; ACTS 1:6-11

Wind and Fire

Jesus' special friends were all together on a special feast day called Pentecost.

Then suddenly . . . there was a wind—a strong wind, a strong and mighty wind, a strong and mighty rushing wind, a strong and mighty rushing wind that filled the whole house.

WHOOOOOOSH!

And then suddenly . . . there were little flames— safe, bright little flames that didn't burn but touched everyone's heads.

"Wow!" everyone said, feeling very excited and happy. "Let's praise God! Let's tell God how much we love him! He's filling us up with his love! Now we can talk in other languages! We can understand other languages!

We can tell everyone about our friend Jesus and how special he is and how much he wants everyone to be his friend."

A big crowd gathered outside the house.

"What is going on?" asked the people in the crowd.

"They must be drunk! They're talking nonsense!"

Then Peter stood up and told the people all about Jesus, God's Son, who had come to save them.

"God's Spirit has come," Peter said. "It is just as God promised long ago. He is always with us, helping us in all we do."

ACTS 2:1-41

Power for the Church

God helped Peter and John and his other friends to be bold and brave. He helped them to be powerful and peaceful.

Peter spoke to the crowds of people.

"Jesus is God's Son," said Peter. "He loves you and died for you. He is the Lord and the King. You must stop doing wrong things and ask him to forgive you."

A lot of people listened to Peter together. They learned about God together. They praised God and prayed together. They had meals together. They cared and shared together.

God helped them make sick people well again. Jesus' friends weren't afraid anymore. They knew that God was always with them, even though he is invisible, like the wind. ACTS 2:14-47; 4:32-37

A New Follower of Jesus

A man named Saul hated all the new Christians.

"Bah! You're all wrong. Go away!" he said.

One day Saul was going along a road to

a city called Damascus. He planned to hurt people who followed Jesus in that city.

Suddenly there was a bright light all around Saul. The light was so bright that he couldn't see, and he fell to the ground. Then Saul heard a voice.

It was Jesus!

"When you hurt the people who love me, you're hurting me, too," said Jesus.

After that Saul became quite different. He wanted Jesus to be his friend. Now he wanted to be a Christian too!

"I'm such a different person," said Saul.

He even chose to be called a different name. "From now on I will be Paul," he said.

Paul joined the Christians and shared the work of telling everyone about Jesus. He was just as excited to help them as he had been to stop them. News spread everywhere about God's love and forgiveness. Soon people in many places were baptized and started to follow and worship Jesus. ACTS 9:1-31; 13:4-12

Peter in Prison

Peter told everyone about how much God loved them. He told them that Jesus had died and risen again so that everyone could be God's friend and live with him in heaven one day.

But there were people who didn't like what Peter said. Peter was put in prison and chained up between two guards.

"Let's pray for Peter," said Peter's friends one night. Together, in Mary's house, they prayed to God.

Meanwhile, Peter was sleeping peacefully in prison. Suddenly an angel was there with Peter, and the prison cell was full of light!

"Wake up!" said the angel. "Get dressed and follow me."

The chains fell off of Peter's wrists, and he followed the angel out of the prison. The prison guards didn't notice him, and the big iron gates swung open for him. Peter went straight to Mary's house, where all his friends were gathered.

Knock, knock, knock! Peter knocked on the door.

A girl named Rhoda answered.

"It's Peter! It's Peter!" she shouted. She was so excited she forgot to let him in!

Knock, knock, knock! Peter tried again.

This time everyone rushed to the door. When his friends saw it really was Peter, they praised God. He had answered their prayers. ACTS 12:1-16

Shipwreck!

Paul and his friends had many adventures. They traveled a lot and made many journeys to tell people all about Jesus.

Sometimes their journeys were dangerous. Sometimes their journeys were long. Sometimes their journeys were on boats in the sea. Sometimes Paul was put in prison for telling about Jesus.

"I want to go to Rome to see the king," said Paul. "He's important and fair, and I'm sure he'll let me stay out of prison. Then I can keep telling people about Jesus."

So Paul and his friends sailed to Rome. At first the sea was calm, but then the wind blew harder! The ship rocked and tipped up and down, up and down in the big waves. But God took care of Paul and his friends.

"God will keep us safe. We won't drown," said Paul.

Then the boat crashed on the shore, just off the island

of Malta. But no one on the boat drowned. The people in Malta welcomed the shipwrecked sailors and looked after them until it was safe for them to sail to Rome again.

Then Paul stayed in a house in Rome and wrote letters to all his friends, teaching them about Jesus, even though he was a long way from them. ACTS 27–28

Paul Writes Some Letters

Paul wrote letters to Christians in some of the places he had visited.

He wrote to tell them that he often thought about them and asked God to take care of them.

He wrote to thank them for making him feel welcome.

He wrote to tell them that God loved them so much that he had sent Jesus to save them.

He wrote to remind them that none of them were perfect and they all needed God's forgiveness.

He wrote to remind them to love God, not just today but every day.

He wrote to tell them to be kind to each other and to share what they had with other people.

At the end of one of his letters he wrote, "God is great and full of glory forever!" ROMANS; 1 AND 2 CORINTHIANS; GALATIANS; EPHESIANS; PHILIPPIANS; COLOSSIANS; 1 AND 2 THESSALONIANS; 1 AND 2 TIMOTHY; TITUS; PHILEMON

No More Tears

After Jesus had risen from the dead, a man named John, who loved God very much, was sent to live on an island in the middle of the sea. The island was called Patmos.

While he was there, he wrote a letter to some other people who loved God. This is what he said:

"God is pure, and God is holy.

"God is good, and God is true and fair.

"God is mighty, and God is holy, holy, holy.

"He will live and rule forever.

"All the angels and every creature will worship him forever and ever."

Then John heard loud trumpets in the starry skies. He saw a sparkling, flowing river and tree-lined streets. He imagined

a wonderful heavenly city shining like the sun. It was a holy city, where there would be no more hurt and pain, no more dying, and no more crying. It was a wonderful city, and everyone who lived there could see God living with them. And God would wipe away every tear from their eyes.

John said, "Lord Jesus, come and be with everyone." REVELATION 1; 4; 21–22

Index of Bible Stories

God Made the World (Genesis 1–2) ... 8

Noah Builds a Boat (Genesis 6–9) ... 10

Under the Stars (Genesis 12:1-8; 15) ... 12

Three Visitors (Genesis 18:1-15; 21:1-7) ... 14

Isaac and Rebekah (Genesis 24) ... 16

Joseph and His Brothers (Genesis 37; 39–41:14) ... 18

Dreams Come True (Genesis 41–47) ... 20

Little Baby Moses (Exodus 2:1-10) ... 22

The King Who Said No (Exodus 3–12) ... 24

Follow the Leader (Exodus 13:17–17:7; 19–20) ... 26

The Best Way to Live (Exodus 20:1-21) ... 28

Joshua's Big Battle (Joshua 1; 3; 6) ... 30

God Chooses Gideon (Judges 6–7; 8:28) ... 32

Ruth and Naomi (Ruth 1–4) ... 34

The Voice in the Night (1 Samuel 1; 3:1-14) ... 36

Seven Sons and a Shepherd Boy (1 Samuel 16:1-13) ... 38

David and Goliath (1 Samuel 17) ... 40

David the Songwriter (Psalm 23) ... 42

Solomon (1 Kings 3; 5–8) ... 44

Elijah and the Ravens (1 Kings 17) ... 46

Fire on the Mountain (1 Kings 18) ... 48

A Dip in the River (2 Kings 5:1-19) ... 50

Jonah Runs the Other Way (Jonah 1–3) ... 52

The Sound of Music (Daniel 1; 3) ... 54

Plots and Plans and Lions (Daniel 6) ... 56

The Promise of a King (Isaiah 9:1-7; 11:1-9; 55:12-13) ... 58

A Visitor for Mary (Luke 1:26-55) ... 60

A Ride to Bethlehem (Luke 2:1-7) ... 62

The Shepherds' Surprise (Luke 2:8-20) ... 64

Follow the Star (Matthew 2:1-12) ... 66

Jesus Gets Lost (Luke 2:41-52) ... 68

Jesus Is Baptized (Matthew 3) ... 70

Jesus' Prayer (Matthew 6:5-13) ... 72

God Cares about You (Matthew 6:25-33; 10:29-31) . . . 74

Very Special Friends (Matthew 4:18-22; 9:9; 10:1-8) . . . 76

Miracle at the Wedding (John 2:1-11) . . . 78

The Hole in the Roof (Luke 5:17-26) . . . 80

The Story of Two Houses (Luke 6:47-49) . . . 82

The House That Fell Down (Luke 6:47-49) . . . 84

The Storm at Sea (Luke 8:22-25) . . . 86

Little Miss Jairus (Luke 8:40-42, 49-56) . . . 88

The Enormous Picnic (John 6:1-13) . . . 90

The Story of the Kind Stranger (Luke 10:25-37) . . . 92

Trouble in the Kitchen (Luke 10:38-42) . . . 94

The Story of the Lost Sheep (Luke 15:3-7) . . . 96

The Loving Father (Luke 15:11-24) . . . 98

The Man Who Couldn't See (Mark 10:46) . . . 100

Help Me! (Mark 10:47-52) . . . 102

The Man Who Climbed a Tree (Luke 19:1-10) . . . 104

Jesus Rides a Donkey (Matthew 21:1-9) . . . 106

Less but More (Luke 21:1-4) . . . 108

A Lonely Garden (Matthew 26:17-30, 36-57) . . . 110

Three Crosses (Luke 23:32-49) . . . 112

A Sad Garden (Matthew 27:57-61; John 19:38-42) . . . 114

A Happy Garden (Luke 24:1-12; John 20:1-18) . . . 116

Two Friends along the Road (Luke 24:13-34) . . . 118

Jesus and Thomas (Luke 24:35-49; John 20:19-29) . . . 120

Breakfast on the Shore (John 21:1-19) . . . 122

Jesus Goes to Heaven (Luke 24:50-52; Acts 1:6-11) . . . 124

Wind and Fire (Acts 2:1-41) . . . 126

Power for the Church (Acts 2:14-47; 4:32-37) . . . 128

A New Follower of Jesus (Acts 9:1-31; 13:4-12) . . . 130

Peter in Prison (Acts 12:1-16) . . . 132

Shipwreck! (Acts 27-28) . . . 134

Paul Writes Some Letters (various New Testament books) . . . 136

No More Tears (Revelation 1; 4; 21-22) . . . 138

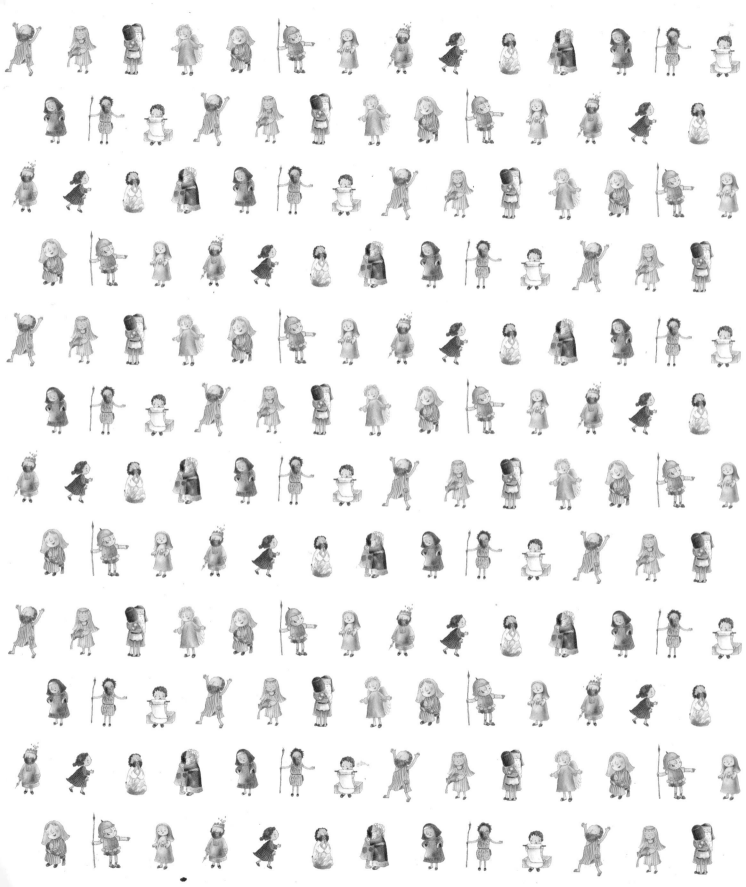